Save Money
Build Wealth

I0033762

OTHER BOOKS BY
DAN CHRISTIAN YEUNG

Dealership Deceit

Save Money Build Wealth

Find Lost Money from Your Everyday Expenses and Pave Your Way to Financial Freedom

DAN CHRISTIAN YEUNG

dan@savemoneybuildwealth.com

Copyright © 2016 by Dan Christian Yeung (*savemoneybuildwealth.com*)

All Rights Reserved. No part of this book may be reproduced, transmitted or distributed in any form or by any means, electrical or mechanical, including photocopying and recording, or by any information storage or retrieval system without permission in writing from *savemoneybuildwealth.com*.

ISBN: 978-0-9947715-1-3

Published by 10-10-10 Publishing
Markham, ON
Canada

The information contained in this book is provided 'as is' without warranty of any kind. The entire risk as to the results and the performance of the information is assumed by the user, and in no event shall *savemoneybuildwealth.com* be liable for any consequential, incidental or direct damages suffered in the course of using the information in this book.

To my wife, Thy, and to my daughter, Rachel.

Contents

Acknowledgements

First of all, I would like to thank Raymond Aaron and his 10-10-10 program for providing me with the confidence and the tools I needed to share my wisdom and experience with the world. I would also like to acknowledge his book architects and staff, Jennifer Le, Jen Morpaw, Andrew Brooke, Helen Everett, Liz Ventrella, and Lisa Browning for providing me with the help and support required to write this book.

I would also like to thank Francis Ablola for being a wonderful mentor to me and inspiring me to kickstart my career.

I would like to thank Miranda Regan for doing an amazing job editing and formatting this book and making it look as amazing as it does.

I would like to thank Jeffery Leung for getting me started on my real estate investing career. I would also like to thank Scott McGillivary, Michael Sarracini, Corey Young, Tiffany Young, and Warren Pratt with Keyspire as well as Marc Mousseau for teaching me what I currently know about real estate investing.

I would like to thank Bob Proctor, Jack Canfield, Loral Langemeier, and Robert Kiyosaki for getting me to believe in myself and for teaching me some of the most inspiring and important wealth principles so I can share them with the readers of this book.

Congratulations!

You're to be commended on taking the first step towards achieving your financial goals, whatever they may be. You see most people desire financial freedom. Most people desire to be rich. The problem is that 99% of the people out there who want to be rich don't take action. They dream about being rich, but they don't do anything about it. They don't change their habits or their actions. Unless you're planning to win the lottery, you can't expect to make more money or work fewer hours if you don't do anything differently than you currently doing. If you're not willing to invest time into reading books, taking courses, engaging a mentor, and other ways of moving forward, your situation's not going to change.

But you're not part of that group. By deciding to pick up this book and start reading it, you're already part of the 1% who are actually willing to take action! So that in itself deserves a lot of praise.

Introduction

How the book is laid out

Save Money, Build Wealth is divided into two different, almost opposite sections, yet complete understanding of both of these sections is vital if you're seeking financial freedom.

The first section deals with saving money. Saving money is an essential habit that you need to develop if you want to be rich. But, I'm not going to tell you to do this by cutting down on your Starbucks purchases. I'm going to tell you how to save money while buying what you're already buying. The key to this section is that you *do not change your spending habits*. (I'll give you a disclaimer later on, but the exception to this is that, if you're spending significantly more than you're bringing in, you might need to alter your spending habits). I'm not going to tell you to stop buying that daily four-dollar latte; I'm going to tell you how to buy that four-dollar latte so you're saving money in the process.

> "I'm not going to tell you to stop buying that daily four-dollar latte; I'm going to tell you how to buy that four-dollar latte so you're saving money in the process."

Using the techniques in this section will put more cash in your pocket. Please note that this is newfound wealth that you would not otherwise have had if you hadn't met me.

The second section deals with building wealth. I'm going to teach you how to invest that money that you're saving in the first section so you can achieve your financial goals. I'm not going to lie. This is not a get-rich-quick book. I'll discuss a few ways you can get rich "quickly," but that's not the premise of this book. Even most relatively reliable get-rich-quick schemes involve a lot of risk. Getting rich requires patience. Depending on your current financial situation and what your financial goals are, it may take anywhere from two to twenty years for you to achieve your goals using the methods in this book. I'll discuss how you can accelerate this process, but keep in mind I'm telling you how to do this with the newfound money that you didn't have before.

Who this book is for

I wrote this book with the typical part-time worker in mind. I'm talking about a part-time worker who is trying to make it financially while supporting a spouse and kids plus trying to make house and car payments. Does this mean that the advice in this book is not valid if you're not a part-time worker or you're not maintaining a family or household?

Of course not!

But the truth is most American and Canadian families fit into this category. Most of us are trying to juggle a mortgage, utility bills, childcare expenses, and car payments on one or two measly salaries. And, as you've probably noticed, the cost of living keeps going up and up, but our income holds steady. Any increases in our income get gobbled up by the increased cost of childcare, groceries, and utilities. We already have to work miracles just to keep our expenses low enough to meet what we make.

But what does this mean?

The problem with having to work miracles just to keep your expenses low enough to meet your income is that you never get to live the life you want. You never get to live in the house that you want to live in. You never drive the car you want to drive. You don't get to take the vacations you want to take. You're almost always overworked and burnt out. With what you have already going on, you never have the time to take any courses or read any books that will help you get ahead financially.

Well, we're going to change that.

Before we go too much further, I just want to mention that there's a very good chance these techniques will work for you. However, I'm also assuming that you are earning close to or a bit more than your expenses. If you're in massive debt or you're spending way more than you're currently making, then I would consider working through a debt elimination program. Check out *savemoneybuildwealth. com/debtelimiation* for the program I'd recommend.

In this book I'll teach you how to save money and build wealth without cutting back your lifestyle. However, if you're in a lot of debt that you need to get out of, the techniques mentioned in this book may work, but you also may need to take a look at cutting back your spending, at least when you're first starting out.

How to use the advice in this book
(hint: TAKE ACTION)

You've probably heard this before, but there's two types of people in this world. There's the type who takes action, and there's the type that doesn't. The type of people who do not take action live their lives by rules set for them by the people who do take action. They're heavily influenced by their

"The type of people who do not take action live their lives by rules set for them by the people who do take action."

environments and the people that surround them. They tend not to think for themselves, and they believe what other people around them tell them to believe. They go through life not knowing why they're here in the first place and generally end up not living a fulfilling life. You can recognize this type of person by how they talk. They're always complaining about something and they mainly talk about things such as news, weather, traffic, and sports.

> **"If you do nothing beyond just reading this book, you'll already see an improvement in your finances."**

Then there's the type of people who take action. I already know that you fit into this category because you've taken the initiative to read this book. This book is chock-full of advice that will create wealth just by rearranging your spending habits. If you do nothing beyond just reading this book, you'll already see an improvement in your finances. You'll learn about new ways to buy what you're already buying as well as ways to invest. You'll subconsciously start putting some of the tips and tricks into action.

But, if you want to get the most out of this book, consciously heed this advice. Do everything that I tell you to do, and then read the books that I tell you to read at the end of this book. You risk little using the tips in the first section, and the second section deals with how to invest the money that you've acquired in the first section, money that you would've otherwise not had if you hadn't picked up this book.

Why you're reading this book

My goal is that by the time you complete this book you'll be armed with the tools and knowledge to keep the lifestyle that you currently have but to still massively increase and accelerate your net worth.

But I'm not sure yet what *your* goal is. Do *you* know what your goal is? Is your goal to have enough money to be comfortable, is your goal to be a millionaire, or is your goal to become the next Steve Jobs or Elon Musk or Bill Gates? Whatever you financial or personal goal is, I can help you achieve it. I've studied the art of building wealth from some of the greatest masters, and I've woven some of their techniques and teachings into this book.

What I'm asking you to do won't be very hard, but I'm going to ask you to build and stick to habits. This is where the magic is. Build and stick to the habits that I'm telling you to build.

Going back to the previous point, the biggest difference I have observed between the people who are wealthy and successful and those who are just getting by is that successful people take action.

I can't say this enough. TAKE ACTION! Build the habits I'm telling you to build and stick to them! I know this will be difficult for you to do at first, but stay with me. It'll be worth it in the end.

Why you should grab that 100 dollar bill

About taking action, one of my mentors, Jack Canfield (co-founder of the *Chicken Soup for the Soul Series*) has an amazing way of teaching this principle. Whenever he gives a speech about how to become wealthy, after giving his spiel about how wealthy and successful people take action, he likes to stand at the front of the stage and hold out a $100 bill. He then asks, "Who would like a $100 bill?" Afterwards, he just stands there. Almost everyone in the room yells, "Me, me, ME!" They wave their hands frantically. Eventually one person will get up, run to the front of the room, and grab the $100 bill from Jack's hand. That person is $100 richer because that person took action. Everyone else in the room yelled out their desire to become $100 richer, but the one person who stood up and took action actually became richer.

Think about that for a minute. Why did it take a while for someone to finally get up and grab it? What thoughts do you think went through everyone's mind? (This is weird, I was waiting for further instructions, others need it more than me, and other defeating thoughts.)

Think about your life and the opportunities that have come by. Were there times you had the chance to become richer appear right in front of you, but rather than getting up and grabbing the opportunity, you just stood by and yelled out your desire to become wealthy (or did nothing)?

Not just rich people, but successful people take action. If you want to be one of these people, taking action is DEFINITELY one of the habits you'll want to build.

Free extras

Ah, yes, these lessons don't stop when this book ends (unless you want them to). *Savemoneybuildwealth.com* has tons of free extras, including:

- A free $10,000 blueprint
- Up-to-date and current articles on how to save money not found in this book
- New ways to invest your newfound money not found in this book
- Other unadvertised extras!

Visit *savemoneybuildwealth.com* on a regular basis so you can keep up-to-date, with new articles and techniques that'll teach you how to further build and grow your wealth. Or better yet, subscribe to my mailing list, and I'll notify you whenever a new article is posted on *savemoneybuildwealth.com*. Remember what I said about people who take action vs. those who don't? Just a gentle heads up, I love to reward those who take action.

Summary

Okay, hopefully you have a taste of what's to come in this book.

I've also already harped on a very important wealth principle. No matter what your goal is, not just in the financial arena, but in ANY arena, taking action is one of the most important habits you can develop. Other habits are also important, but I'll get into those as we go along.

Also, remember, if you're carrying a significant amount of debt or your expenses are substantially larger than your income, take action and enroll in a debt elimination program. You can find one at *savemoneybuildwealth.com/debt-elimination*. The rest of these principles may work for you, but they'll be much more effective if you take care of your debt first.

In the next section I'll get into how you can save money by doing what you're already doing.

Section 1:
Save Money

Overview

As mentioned before, I'm going to start with teaching you how to save money by doing what you're already doing. If all you're looking for is money-saving tips, just skip to page 25 or, better yet, visit and subscribe to *savemoneybuildwealth.com*.

But if you want to make this program work for you and increase your net worth in the process, read the entire chapter. You need to do a few things before you leap into action.

First, you need to figure out where you are. I keep saying that I don't want you to cut back your lifestyle and your standard of living, but what does your current lifestyle look like? Well, we need to figure that out.

Next, you're going to open a wealth account. I'm going to tell you want kind of account you need to open and how much money to put into it and how often. As you can probably guess, the money you put in is money that you're saving using the techniques mentioned in this chapter and on *savemoneybuildwealth.com*. But how often should you be moving money into this account? And what are we going to call this account? The name you give this account is pivotal to the amount of money that will eventually be in it.

Lastly, I'll list some ways you can save money in your everyday life. I've included a pretty good list, but I definitely suggest that you visit *savemoneybuildwealth.com* for a more updated list. I also highly recommend you subscribe to *savemoneybuildwealth.com* so you're notified once a new article is posted.

Sound good? Okay, let's move on!

How to make this section work for you

"To change your life, you need to change your life." – Bob Proctor

You are where you are right now because of the decisions and actions that you've taken so far. The great Bob Proctor, self-made millionaire and star of the movie *The Secret*, also mentions that if you want to change your circumstances or change your life, you need to "change your life." I know this sounds like a play on words, but it's true if you think about it. If you don't change your daily routine, your circumstances will not change. Some of the stuff that I'm going to tell you might sound strange. But it's going to sound strange because it's stuff you're not used to doing and that the people you spend time with on a regular basis are not used to doing.

I'm going to go into detail about this later on, but we're heavily influenced by our environment. Part of the reason that you don't know to do some of the things that I'm going to tell you to do and part of the reason I'm going to tell you to do some "strange" things is

"We're heavily influenced by our environment."

because your environment or conditioning is telling you that it's strange. But remember, your environment and conditioning is what got you to where you are right now.

I hang out regularly with some of the wealthiest and most successful people in the world. And the stuff that I'm going to tell you to do that seems strange to you and the people in your environment wouldn't seem strange to those successful people at all. They'll even credit some of that stuff to their success.

Getting back on topic, I need you to read this section and the rest of this book with an open mind. Then, I need you to buy into some of the stuff that I'm telling you to do. If some of the stuff feels awkward, just try it out for a month. If it's not helping, then stop doing it. But I need you to try it. Remember what I said about taking action? Yes, running to the stage to grab the $100 bill will feel strange and awkward (that's why no one's doing it) but the person who worked past that awkwardness (or didn't feel awkward doing it) is the one who's $100 richer.

What if I just read it and do nothing else?

You know, our subconscious mind is a funny thing. I am making the assumption here that you do indeed desire to learn ways of saving money without changing your spending habits. Well, if all you do is read this book, then you'll already have put this into action without thinking about it! Well, you'll be subconsciously thinking about it. After reading this section, whenever you fill up your car or go to the grocery store, you'll watch yourself employing these techniques without even trying!

Why? Because just by reading this book you're programing your subconscious mind. For instance, you're programing your mind to change the way you buy groceries to a way that's cheaper and more efficient than the way you're currently doing it. I'm going to make you aware of better ways of going about it. But, once you have the awareness, as long as you keep referring to this book and the articles on *savemoneybuildwealth.com*, you're going to subconsciously keep employing the methods in this book, which means more money for you.

95% of the things you do you're doing because you're programmed to do it. You're programed to walk the way you walk, talk the way you talk, dress the way you dress. You were programmed to wake up at a certain time and perform a certain ritual. There's a ritual to everything you do. There's a ritual to everything *I* do. If you wake up in the morning and put a different leg into your pants first than the one you normally put in, you'll probably fall over.

Of all the things we do in a given day, only 5% of the things we do we're consciously doing. The rest we do subconsciously, and unless you're deliberately programming your subconscious mind to do things a certain way, you're doing it the way other people are doing it.

What does this mean? Ultimately, if you read this section, and read it more than once, you'll ultimately subconsciously start saving money without any conscious effort. Neat, eh?

Summary

Okay, so we've covered some introductory points regarding how to make this section work for you and what you can expect. We've also touched a bit on how we're all programed to do what we do. The next chapter will delve deep into the mindset you need to adopt and then I'll get you started on some transactional stuff. (I'm going to explain what a "Transactional Change" and a "Transformational Change" are in the next chapter.) Before I can help you squeeze money out of your everyday purchases, I'll need you to change your mindset. I'll need to debunk some myths and get you to see yourself as deserving of more money and a better lifestyle. You might not believe this now, but even by picking up this book, you deserve way more money and a way better lifestyle than 98% of the other people in your life who have not decided to do something about their life.

What to Do?

Change your mindset

There are two different types of change that can happen to you:

- Type 1: Transactional Change
- Type 2: Transformational Change

A Transactional Change is an external change. It means that you do something differently than you've been doing before in the external world (i.e. you take the bus instead of the taxi to get to work this morning).

A Transformational Change can be external as long as it's a HUGE change (you quit your job and start your own business) or you make a fundamental internal change to a core habit or belief (you stop thinking about and focusing on debt and instead spend all your energy focusing on how to generate automatic wealth and income).

Raymond Aaron, one of my mentors, teaches people like you how to double their income doing what you love in, appropriately, his book called *Double Your Income Doing What You Love*. He does some very powerful stuff to accelerate his students' incomes and teaches some mind-blowing principles. What he does is transformational. Transformational Changes result in a 100% to 1000% increase in your income. Transformational Changes also require massive changes to your paradigms.

Bob Proctor defines paradigms as a multitude of habits. To get the most out of *Save Money, Build Wealth*, a Transformational Change needs to occur in your subconscious mind. Reading a list of ways to save money is "Transactional." Transactional Changes only result in a 5% to 50% increase in your income. Which is fine, but I'm guessing you're here for a Transformational Change.

Back to this. You need to adopt a different mindset. You need to be willing to change your habits and beliefs.

But change it to what?

What am I currently believing that I need to change?

You're currently earning what you're earning because you're programmed to do so. You're saving what you're currently saving (if anything) because you are programmed to do so.

"Apparently 98% of all lottery winners spend their winnings within the first five years."

I heard an alarming but unsurprising statistic on the radio the other day. Apparently 98% of all lottery winners spend their winnings within the first five years. And many of them end up declaring bankruptcy.

Why is that?

Again, programming. Most people are where they are because they were programmed. They're programmed to earn what they currently earn and spend what they currently spend. Add an immediate $10M or $20M shot without a transformational change, and guess what? Many lottery winners are programmed to only earn $50,000 a year and spend $50,000 a year with nothing left in savings. In order to get back to that equilibrium, these people will buy a house, buy houses for all their friends, buy a boat, luxury vacation, fancy car, jet, and lots of other high cost items. How do you think a person like this will feel when the money's gone?

Why am I going through all this? Because, you're going to have newfound money, but if you don't change your paradigms your current paradigms will kick in, and you'll probably not be any further ahead than before you started reading this book. And I don't want that. I need you to have a transformational change. I want you to start believing that you are worthy of being wealthy and worthy of actually living the life you want to live.

Don't cut back on your lifestyle

"You can't move forward when you're cutting back." – Bob Proctor

When the average person starts running into financial difficulty, she cuts back her spending to meet her income. When a wealthy person starts running into financial difficulty, the wealthy person elevates her income to meet her standard of living. My core focus in this book isn't to discuss how to elevate your income, but I discuss some ways of doing so at the end.

You're reading this book likely because you want to build wealth. It is, after all, in the title. Well, what I can tell you is that you can't "save" your way to financial freedom. Building wealth requires creativity, and cutting back on your lifestyle will take away from this.

Decide what your financial goals are

Building wealth is a journey, unless you win the lottery or you're lucky enough to make a "get rich scheme" work. But even then, if you don't alter your paradigms, it'll all be gone just as fast as you acquired it. Weirdly enough, if you take a look at wealthy people (who acquired their wealth outside of a get-rich-quick scheme or lottery), if you take away all their money and possessions, those formerly wealthy people will more likely than not be able to rebuild their wealth.

So, you need to embark on a journey to build wealth. Let's just look at the concept of a journey for a second. You need to know three things in order to have a successful journey:

- Where you are
- Where you want to go (your destination)
- How you are going to get there

Your financial journey is no different. You need to know where you currently are, you need to know what your goal is ($5M net worth, $50,000 per month passive income, or something like this), and how you're going to get there.

Actually, here's a fourth thing that you should know:

- How long are you willing to take to get there

Figuring out where you are is easy enough. I'm going to go through this in a bit. Figuring out where you want to go is another story. Deciding how much money you want to have in retirement or what your financial goals are is outside of the scope of this book, but it would be a great idea to think about this for a bit. If I could give you a moneymaker, how much money would you need to or want to take out of it on a monthly basis? If you had this moneymaker, what would you buy with it? How much would you take out of this to give to charity? Try to figure out how much you need this moneymaker to produce. Try to come up with a rough goal, at least for now.

This book will show you a few ways to get there, but many, many more ways exist. Squeezing extra profits out of your purchases is a very good start, but depending on your goals, you need to transform way beyond this.

Look at how much you currently spend

Okay, now that we talked about changing your mindset and coming up with a goal and roadmap, we need to determine where you currently are. Take out a sheet of paper, and write down what you currently make on a monthly basis. If what you make varies month to month, write down the average of the last twelve months. Be sure to include any other income from other sources such as other jobs or services or rental properties.

Next, you need to determine your expenses. Try to figure out how much you spend on a monthly basis. Take an average of the last twelve months. You can estimate these numbers if you wish. What you need to know is how much you spend on a monthly basis on:

- Rent or mortgage payments
- Car payments
- Childcare
- Water, power, and heating bills
- Gas (for your car or cars)
- Home insurance
- Auto insurance
- Life insurance
- Property taxes
- Interest on lines of credit or credit cards
- Eating out
- Starbucks (or Dunkin' Donuts or Tim Hortons)
- Entertainment (movies, football games, etc.)
- Groceries
- Cellphone bills

And any other reoccurring expenses I didn't mention.

If you bring in more than 10% of what you spend, you're doing very well! Hopefully you're already saving and investing that money.

If you go ahead and do this exercise, you'll already have cut down on your spending. You'll have shed light on some of your expenses, and you'll subconsciously trim down some of them. I swear, every time I mention this exercise, I notice that I cut down on eating out and Starbucks. Sometimes all it takes is shedding light on some of you expenditures.

But remember, I don't want you to cut down on your expenditures (unless you absolutely have to). This is just a starting point. I want you to have these reoccurring expenditures, but I want you to buy these items in a different way, and I want you to do something special with the money you're saving.

Open a $10,000 bank account

The next step is: Open a dedicated bank account. On my website, I tell you to call this a $10,000 account, and actually that's not a bad idea at all. I tell you to call it a $10,000 account because I want you to get used to having $10,000 in your account. I fully realize that you likely don't have $10,000 to put in it **right now**, but you will sometime in the future. And you don't have to call it your $10,000 account. You can be ambitious and call it a $25,000 account or a $100,000 account as well. But, please ensure that you use a number at or higher than $10,000.

Why are you calling this a $10,000 account?

Ah, we're back to this mindset stuff. By consistently calling this a $10,000 account, or $25,000 account, or whatever your goal may be, you'll subconsciously do what you need to do in order to have $10,000 in it. Calling this a $10,000 account when it has less than $10,000 causes a subconscious incongruity that your subconscious mind relentlessly tries to resolve. A simple savings or checking account will do for now because they're quick and easy to open and I want to get you started on this as soon as possible.

Can I use an existing account?

Only if you're not using it for anything else. This is where your newfound wealth is going. The only transactions that should be happening are either money is going into it or money is going out of it to buy *assets*. I'm going to define "asset" in the wealth-building part of this book. Also, just a heads-up that your $10,000 account is not going to be a savings account forever. I'll need you to eventually apply for and open up a brokerage account. Once money starts rolling in, you're going to need to use that money to make more money.

Summary

We're all set up! Hopefully you took action and either opened up a new $10,000 account or converted an existing account that you're not using into a $10,000 account. Hopefully you've also heeded all that mindset advice and have committed to taking on new habits that will get you to achieve your financial goals. I haven't explicitly spelled this out yet, but ultimately you have to take full 100% responsibility for your results. That's actually Jack Canfield's first principle in his book *The Success Principles: How to Get from Where You Are to Where You Want to Be*. If you blame other people or circumstances for you not taking action, it's akin to blaming a chair for blocking your way to running up and grabbing that $100 bill. Blame all you want, but it was your choice not to go and grab it, or in this case, not going to the bank and opening up a $10,000 account.

I've focused a lot on this mindset stuff because I need you to undergo a Transformational Change before we can make good use of the transactional stuff. The next chapter goes into how much money you should be putting into your $10,000 account and ways to save money in your everyday life. Putting money into this account takes discipline though, and you'll need to form a new habit. If you're like many and you're not used to putting money into a savings account on a regular basis, committing to and forming this habit is CRUCIAL. Robert Kiyosaki, author of *Rich Dad, Poor Dad* and probably the best known wealth coach, says that one of the biggest differences between wealthy people and average people is that wealthy people pay themselves **first** and average people pay themselves **last**. I know it's tough to save some of your income when there's nothing left after your expenses, but I'm going to ask you to save money that you didn't have access to before. In essence, you're going to be saving money that you didn't have in the first place, and you won't need to cut back any of your expenses! Excited? Keep reading!

How to Save Money

"Anything that can be measured can be improved"
Francis Ablola, Author of The Art and Science of Success,
Proven Strategies from Today's Leading Experts

As mentioned earlier, just by reading this chapter you're going to save money on your everyday purchases without any conscious effort. All these lists, as well as other more up-to-date information, can be found at *savemoneybuildwealth.com*. It'd be a great idea for you to subscribe as well so you can be informed when a new list or article is posted on s*avemoneybuildwealth.com*.

But, I also need to tell you how much money to put into your $10,000 account.

Option 1:

At the end of each month, add up how much you've spent. There are three possible outcomes:

- Outcome 1 - You've spent less than you normally spend on a monthly basis
- Outcome 2 - You've spent exactly what you normally spend on a monthly basis
- Outcome 3 - You've spent more than what you normally spend on a monthly basis

If Outcome 1 applies for you for the month, put the difference between what you would normally spend on a monthly basis and what you actually spent that month into your $10,000 account.

Do this at the beginning of every month!

You need to build the habit of putting money into your $10,000 account.

What if outcome 2 or 3 applies this month?

Then transfer $1 into your $10,000 account.

Your habits and mindset are what will make you wealthy, not the actual money you make on a given month. Especially if you've never done this before, you need to get used to putting money into a savings account *every month*, even if you don't have any money to save in a given month.

You need to be dedicated to this. You need to feel guilty if it's the beginning of the month and you haven't done this yet.

Why the beginning of the month?

I also need you to program your subconscious to pay yourself first. This needs to feel like it's your "first priority," not your last. This goes back to our wealth principle mentioned in the previous chapter: pay yourself first, not last. Actually, what I do is as soon as I receive payment for any of the services that are provided is 10% goes into my $10 million account, 10% goes to charity, and 20% goes to debt repayment. I then do whatever I want with the other 60%. If you do have the flexibility to do this, this model will get you to financial freedom pretty quickly. If you do not have the ability to save any of your income right now, you should be able to squeeze out some money using the tips in the next section. But you need to build a "pay yourself first" habit. Since most people do monthly budgets and I've asked you to do a monthly budget in the previous section, it only makes sense that you pay yourself at the beginning of each month.

Option 2:

Another way to go about this—though I don't recommend it as

much as Option 1—is when you cash in a free drink or sub, put the money you would have spent on that item into your $10,000 account. Also, when you're about to pay your utility bill, and you notice that your utility bill is lower than usual, you put the difference into your $10,000 account. While this method does work, it doesn't align with the "pay yourself first" habit that I want you to build.

How to save money with generic brands

You will be able to find updated versions of these articles as well as other articles at savemoneybuildwealth.com. *This is just a sampling to get you started.*

Before we go on, I just want to talk a little bit about store brands versus national brands. By this I mean the difference between buying Heinz ketchup and buying a generic Costco brand or Walmart brand or Kmart brand ketchup.

A lot of the brands that you'll see in a supermarket such as soap, laundry detergent, shampoo, and other household items are owned by one of three companies—Procter & Gamble, Johnson & Johnson, and Unilever. These three companies own brands such as Dawn, Dove, Popsicle, Sunlight, and Tylenol. At the supermarket, you'll likely notice that the supermarket also offers their own version of soap, laundry detergent, and shampoo. Who do you think manufactures the supermarket brand soap and laundry detergent?

Believe it or not, the same guys who make the Costco brand of laundry detergent are the same guys who make Tide. So, if you're at Costco and you see the Costco brand of laundry detergent sitting beside the Tide laundry detergent, and you make the decision to buy the Tide version because you think it's better in quality or cleaning power than the Costco version, you're actually making the decision to pay more for the same product. Tide made the Costco brand. It's the same stuff! The reason why Procter & Gamble (owners of the Tide brand) do this is

27

through commercials and advertising they can get people to spend more money on the brand-name product rather than saving money on the supermarket version of the product. The reason why they also offer the Costco version of this product is because they know there is a segment of the market that doesn't care what brand their laundry detergent is as long as it is laundry detergent. If Costco only offered the Tide brand, they and Procter & Gamble would lose out on a potential sale.

So, the next time you visit Walmart and you're faced with the decision of whether to buy the Walmart brand ketchup or Heinz ketchup, remember that both ketchups were made in the same facility.

…But the brand name stuff tas es better!

Actually it's the same stuff. Companies spend billions of dollars on radio and TV and print ads to convince you that the branded stuff tastes better, but it is indeed the exact same stuff.

I'll give you an example here. There are two major manufacturers of soda or pop. As you probably know one of them is Coca-Cola and the other one is Pepsi. Back in the 1980s, in an effort to gain market share, Pepsi started doing taste tests. This turned ultimately into a commercial campaign where Pepsi proved that in blind taste tests their soft drink tastes better than Coca-Cola. You may be very familiar with this commercial campaign.

But what you're probably not familiar with is the sighted taste test. Pepsi ran a very similar campaign except it wasn't a blind taste test; participants got to see what they were sampling. The result of this campaign showed that Coca-Cola "tasted better" than Pepsi.

So, why do you think that in a **blind** taste test Pepsi tastes better than Coca-Cola, but in a **sighted** taste test, Coca-Cola "tastes better" than Pepsi? Coca-Cola has a much larger marketing budget. Pepsi tastes better than Coca-Cola, but people prefer Coca-Cola and think Coca-Cola tastes better than Pepsi because Coca-Cola is better branded. Heinz ketchup is way better branded than Costco ketchup. Heinz spends tens of millions of dollars per year on marketing, and Costco doesn't even advertise. People will swear that Heinz ketchup tastes better than Costco ketchup because Heinz does a better job branding their ketchup than Costco.

Now, does this mean that the store brand is always cheaper than the brand name version of the same product? The truth is sometimes you'll find that if you compare the price per weight between the brand name and store brand versions of the same product, you'll find that the brand name version can be cheaper than the store brand. Remember to compare products based on price per weight, not total price!

I know it'll be tough, at least at first, but you'll save a ton of money if you switch over from buying brand name items to generic items when you shop for groceries. This switch has the potential to save you at least 20-30% on your grocery bill.

How to save money without altering your lifestyle

How do the words "saving money" sound to you? Not very positive, are they? Most people think of reducing the amount of times they eat out or visit Starbucks or even sitting around in the cold or the dark! Well, there are tricks and simple little changes that you can do to reduce the amount of money that you spend and not alter your lifestyle! I've a bit of a list here, but this is by no means exhaustive.

And you know what? You don't need to make a point to go out and make any of these changes! Even just by studying this list, believe it or not, you'll automatically implement some of the things on this list. You know what that means?

You'll save money without even trying!

Don't believe me? I challenge you. Read this list carefully, but don't make it a point to go out and do anything on it. See if you don't find yourself, all of the sudden, taking a bottle or a snack with you when you go out, or turning down your water heater, or even unplugging your larger electronics when you're not using them.

1. Whenever you go somewhere, take a bottle of water and a snack with you. This will reduce your temptation to buy snacks and drinks elsewhere.

2. Consider buying in bulk. Common household items such as toilet paper, shampoo, soap, cleaning supplies, peanuts, cashews may be purchased bulk at a cheaper price. But remember, always comparison shop the unit price per pound or per ounce or per gram. Sometimes stores try tricking you into paying more by making you think that buying in bulk is cheaper, but that's not always true!

3. Learn how to cook. Take a cooking class. You may just discover on your own that cooking is actually fun! And, without knowing it, you'll be less tempted to eat out, which will in turn mean that you spend less money eating out.

4. Have a freezer? Use it! Whenever you're cooking a meal, make extras, and either leave it in the fridge or the freezer. This will save you more money and the time you would've spent preparing meals for the next day.

5. Never enter a grocery store unless you've already scoured for coupons in their flyers or online. Also, take complete advantage of every supermarket's point system. You shouldn't check out of the supermarket unless you have a points card with you.

6. Consider reusing cloth from clothing that you no longer

wear instead of purchasing disinfecting wipes and towels.

7. Use greywater or collected storm water to water your houseplants and garden. When you take a shower, turn off the water flow when you don't need it. For instance, when you're washing your hair, lathering your body, brushing your teeth.

8. Unplug your electronics when they're not in use. This means your TV, your cable box, your DVD player, cell phone chargers, even possibly your alarm clock. Connecting all these items to a power bar makes this easy. Also, it would be a really good idea to make sure your computer goes into sleep mode when you're not using it.

9. Set the thermostat on your hot water heater to 120°F. Water heaters are installed at the default setting of 140°F; however, in most cases, you can get away with 120°F.

10. Do your laundry in cold water and hang dry your clothes. Not only is this energy efficient (you won't believe how much energy your dryer actually uses), it's actually better for your clothes in the long run because they last longer. This doesn't mean you need to put in a clothesline. You can purchase a dryer rack that you can use in your laundry room.

11. Consider shopping at thrift stores, especially if you're looking for athletic wear, home wear, or something to wear where you not going to be in public or need to look nice. You might even find some nice accessories for cheap as well!

12. Use public transportation when available. If you live near a well-serviced transit stop, whether it be a bus, train, or streetcar stop, take advantage of it! In almost all cases taking public transportation will be cheaper than the cost of the gas and maintenance required to drive your car to the same destination. If public transportation is sparse in your area,

consider carpooling with someone you know.

Remember my challenge.

Don't try to do anything on this list. See what happens. I'll bet you you'll be amazed at how you program your mind to automatically save money.

Don't forget to invest the money you're saving wisely!

How to reduce your home insurance premium

Here are some facts about home insurance:

- **It's mandatory to have if you have a mortgage**
- It's an excellent idea to have it even if you don't have a mortgage
- **95% of Americans and Canadians are GROSSLY OVER-INSURED**

Being grossly over-insured means you're paying for insurance on stuff that either cannot be insured, does not need to be insured, or on stuff THAT DOES NOT EXIST!

And it's costing you tons of money.

You see, most of us don't think twice when we take out a policy. We just call up an insurance company, ask for home insurance, answer the questions they ask, and then pay our monthly bill.

But, take a second look at your policy.

- Do you need to insure yourself against hurricanes if there never has been nor will be a hurricane in your area?
- **Do you need flood protection if you live in the desert?**
- Are you insured for the value of your house PLUS THE

VALUE OF THE LAND YOUR HOUSE IS SITTING ON?

49% Of American homeowners are paying insurance for the land their house is sitting on

Most Americans don't notice this. They think it's good enough to be insured for the full value of their house. They don't notice that they're insured for the land their house is sitting on as well.

But think about it.

Sure, if a tornado comes along and wipes out your house, then it would be nice to be insured for the rebuild cost of your house. But can a tornado or a hurricane come along and wipe out the land your house is sitting on?

How can insurance companies get away with this?

Most Americans do not readtheir home insurance policy!

Most Americans do not know what they're insured for, so insurance companies can pretty much put what they want on their policy (within the laws in your area). But it's up to you, the consumer, to read your policy, and get your insurance company to reduce the coverage on stuff that's too high or remove coverage on stuff that doesn't need to be insured. Like the land your house is sitting on.

By the way, if you're interested, here's seventeen other ways to lower your home insurance premium:

1. Shop around and ask for quotes, at least five different quotes from five different companies. I can't say this enough: In order to get the best rates, you need to shop around!

2. Increase your deductible. Most Americans and Canadians have a deductible of $500, but increasing it to $1000 or even

$2000 can lower your payment by as much as 20%.

3. Don't insure what you don't have.

- If your protection limit is higher than the value of the stuff you actually own, ask for it to be lowered.

- Some homeowners opt to only insure their more valuable possessions. If you do this, take photos and record serial numbers of valuables and keep this information safe and away from your house.

4. Stop smoking.

5. Pay annually instead of monthly.

6. If you work for a company, ask them if they can offer you cheaper insurance through one of their partners.

7. Clean up your credit score.

8. Live in a safe neighborhood close to a fire department and hospital.

9. Live in a neighborhood with a Homeowners' Association (HOA).

10. Make sure there's a fire hydrant close to your house.

11. Buy a newer house over an older house.

12. Stick with the same insurance company for a long time and ask for a loyalty discount.

13. Insure your cars with the same company as your house.

14. If you are retired, ask if you can get a discount; insurance companies assume that retired people tend to spend more time at home.

15. Doing a renovation?

- Update your piping and wiring to meet the most current codes.

- Switch to a natural gas or electric furnace if your house currently uses heating oil or solid fuels.

16. Even if you're not doing a renovation, you still can:

- Install smoke detectors and burglar alarms that automatically notify the authorities when there's an emergency.

- Keep a fire extinguisher in the kitchen.

- Install impact resistant roofing and storm shutters if you live in a storm corridor.

- Install sensors that detect water and gas leaks.

- Install a sewer backflow valve or device.

17. Get a house that fits the area you live in.

- If you live on the East Coast, get a brick home because it's more wind-resistant.

- If you live in an earthquake-prone area, get a wood frame house because it is more likely to withstand earthquakes.

Some reminders:

If you're doing some of the stuff in the above list to lower your insurance premium, tell your insurance company what you did! There's no sense installing a 2-way alarm system in order to lower your insurance premium, and then not tell your insurance company. How are they going to know?

Most basic insurance policies do not cover earthquakes, floods, hurricanes, or tornadoes. If you live in an area which is susceptible to severe weather, make sure you're covered for this stuff.

If you work from home, you should probably tell your insurance company that as well.

Also, please don't blow the money that you're saving. Please invest that money in something smart that will help you build wealth and become financially secure.

How to save on gas

Save as much as 50% on your refueling costs

With fuel prices going up all the time, it becomes harder and more painful to fill up our gas tanks. Sure we're starting to see a switch over to electric cars, but most of the vehicles on the road are still gasoline powered. Even with the recent, temporary, fall in oil prices we're still getting gouged at the pump. Not to worry, I've compiled a list of twelve ways you can reduce the amount of gasoline you need to use:

1. Maintain your car as per the manufacturer's recommendations. A poorly-tuned engine will use 50% more fuel than a properly-tuned engine. Sure, you'll save money by not visiting the mechanic when you're supposed to, but if you end up spending more money on fuel, is it worth it?

2. As mentioned before, take public transit or carpool whenever you can. Having a car is convenient if you need to drive somewhere far off in a reasonable amount of time, but if you don't need to travel as far or if you have a friend that's going to the exact same place you are, doesn't it make sense to tag along? Also, if it takes fifteen minutes to drive where you want to go and the bus also takes fifteen minutes to go where you want to go, consider taking the bus.

3. Drive smoothly and brake faster. I personally love racing movies like *The Fast and the Furious*, but racing against other drivers and stopping and starting quickly not only increases the wear and tear on your car, but consumes as much as 40%

more fuel than if you were driving smoothly (think about how grandma drives). Okay, fine, you don't need to drive like grandma. But at least consider easing off the accelerator once your car is moving so it shifts into high gear earlier.

4. On a related note—use the cruise control! Only use it in good weather conditions. But the cruise control will help you drive more smoothly and keep your fuel usage down.

5. Don't let your vehicle idle for longer than thirty seconds. If you're at a red light or in a moving drive-thru or it's -30 degress outside, idling is fine. But if you're waiting for a long train or you're waiting to pick someone up and it's warm outside, consider turning your car off.

6. Ensure your tires are properly inflated. Underinflated tires will increase your fuel consumption by as much as 6%.

7. Drive in the proper gear. Keeping your car in a lower gear than it should be wastes fuel. But, if you're going up a hill or rounding a corner keeping your car in a higher gear than it needs to be is also bad for your engine.

8. Avoid heavy traffic and traffic lights. Yes, some routes require less driving, but it's actually better if you avoid heavy traffic and avoid traffic lights even if you have to drive a longer distance.

9. Clean your trunk out! Lugging around a messy trunk full of stuff that you don't need will increase your fuel consumption by at least 10%. (This applies to your back seat as well.)

10. Use the correct oil for your car. Using the wrong oil for your car and/or the weather conditions may increase the friction in your engine.

11. Fill up at the correct time. Fill up in the morning or when

the temperature is low. Gasoline is denser when it's colder outside, so you'll be getting more bang for your buck when it's cold. You're charged by the volume not the density.

12. If you have a Costco or Sam's Club membership, fill up there because the gas is cheaper there than at most other locations.

By the way, just an extra tip, if you see a tanker truck refilling the gas station, get gas somewhere else. Dirt and sludge in the underground storage tanks gets stirred up when gas is being delivered, and some of that dirt and sludge will end up in YOUR gas tank.

And there you go. Twelve simple tips that can lower your fuel consumption by as much as 50%!

How to save money at the dealership

If you subscribed to savemoneybuildwealth.com, then you can read a great article on getting a great deal on a car. When you take action, stuff like that happens.

If you didn't, well, see what happens? Nothing. Which is too bad because you could be saving upwards of $10,000 on your next car purchase...

How to save money with reward programs

If you go to Starbucks, or Tim Hortons, or Dunkin' Donuts, or McDonald's, etc., make sure you have a loyalty card, make sure you understand what rewards you'll get for visiting these businesses on a regular basis, and make sure you cash in all these rewards! The cost of "rewarding" customers is already built into the price of their products, but these businesses count on a lot of their customers not taking advantage of the reward program.

For example, Starbucks Canada has a program where every time you buy a drink you get a "star." When you have twelve stars, you can redeem them for a free drink. A lot of times, I notice that regulars at Starbucks don't even have a Starbucks card. They're too lazy or don't want to take the time or effort to sign up for a loyalty card. The problem is though that if you don't make the time to do this, and you drink Starbucks every day, you miss out on the chance to save $10 or even $15 a month.

Yes, I know that $10 or $15 isn't a lot of money, but it adds up. $10 or $15 a month over ten years compounded at 10% is $2,065.52 to $3,098.28. Subway also has a program where if you load $25 onto a gift card, you get a free sub. If you eat at Subway every day, make sure you take advantage of this loyalty program and actually make an effort to use and (almost) abuse the Subway card. This could mean another savings of $10 a month. If you add the $10 a month you're saving from the Starbucks and the Subway cards, that means you will have an extra $4,000 in your $10,000 account over ten years.

What you have to do on an ongoing basis

I know were not dealing with monumental savings here. $100 a month or even $200 a month will not necessarily pave your way to financial freedom, but it's a good start. As you may or may not have guessed, I'm not so focused on how much you're actually putting away; I'm focused on getting you into the *habit* of putting away money. To make you feel better about doing this, I'm having you put away money that you would've otherwise not have discovered had you not met me.

By the way, if you want to be a millionaire, if you're willing to wait twenty-five years, you'll need to invest a little under $350 a month at 15% interest. If you want to do it in ten years, you'll need to find a way to put away a little over $3500 a month at 15% interest.

How you get 15% interest? I'll talk about that in the next section. I'm also going to explain in the next section how to accelerate your wealth if you're interested.

But, in the meantime, I need you to develop the habit of paying yourself first. If you have no way to pay yourself in a given month, pay yourself a dollar. Now that I've shown you how to find extra money in your everyday expenses, you have no excuse not to have some money at the beginning of each month to put away.

It's your paradigms that will make you a millionaire, not necessarily how much money you have right now to put away or invest.

Section 2:
Build Wealth

Open a Brokerage Account

What we're going to call this account
(set a goal)

Congratulations! I commend you for getting this far. Hopefully you've opened up your $10,000 or $25,000 or $100,000 account by now (mine's called a $10 million account; I'm quite ambitious) and hopefully you're putting some money into it at the beginning of every month. If you're doing this, read on!

I'm going to help you increase the amount of money that you have in your account. If you're not putting away money yet, I can't stop you from reading on, but the rest of this information won't be of much use if you haven't developed the habit of paying yourself first.

> **"You need to start getting that money to make more money for you."**

Okay, you have a $10,000 account, which is good. But, unless your checking or savings account is paying you some amazing interest, the money isn't really doing you much good just sitting there. What you need to do is invest it. You need to start getting that money to make more money for you.

See, there are three ways to make money (in his book *Cashflow Quadrant*, Robert Kiyosaki breaks down one of the methods when he talks about four ways of making money). The first way—and this is what 97% of Americans and Canadians do—is to trade time for money. You have a job. You go to work for eight hours a day, and you earn money on a per hour rate. Or, you have a small business, or you're an owner/operator and you get paid for jobs that you do. Mr. Kiyosaki breaks these two methods up, but they're essentially the same—you trade time and effort for money.

The second way is to use money to make more money. You invest it. You lend it or give it to other people, and you get paid interest or a dividend. You know that banks make billions of dollars a year just by lending money to other people? Did you know **you** can do the same thing?

If you have access to a line of credit, you can lend the bank's money out to other people and collect a profit

If you didn't know you can do this, it's because no one ever told you that you have this option. I'll tell you about how to do this later on. Right now though, I'm going to want you to buy Index ETF's (again, explained later) and for you to do this, you'll need what's called a "self-directed brokerage account." Most checking and savings accounts don't necessarily let you buy and hold stocks in them. Brokerage accounts do. Self-directed brokerage accounts let you pick what you want to buy.

Okay, that was a lot of talking to get you to what I want you to do at this step. What I would like you to do is visit *savemoneybuildwealth. com/brokerage-account* and open one up. You'll likely need a social security number or social identification number as well as a driver's license or other ID.

If you're doing this at a bank, the person who opens your account might try to figure out what kind of investor you are (short term, long term, high risk, low risk, or another kind) This person is likely trying to sell you mutual funds on behalf of the bank. I'll talk about this later on, but please don't buy mutual funds! I'll tell you what to invest in next, but if you're in the United States, I'll want you to invest in S&P500 ETF's, and in Canada, I'll want you to invest in either a TSX Index ETF or major bank ETF. More information is coming up shortly though, please be patient. I'll get to all this stuff!

By the way, if you're wondering what the third way is, it's having more than one source of income. It's having a few (or more) rental properties, a few businesses, online marketing income, book royalties, and doing things like speaking engagements and other projects. Only 1% of us are doing this, and as you can imagine, this 1% of the population has 96% of the money.

Regular vs. tax-sheltered

So, you're going to open a brokerage account. But, you have many different types of brokerage accounts to choose from. There are cash accounts, margin accounts, and option accounts. Margins allow you to borrow money to buy stocks and option accounts allow you to buy options. I don't want to get into too much detail about how to buy stocks and options, but quickly an "option" allows you to buy the right to buy a stock when it hits a certain price rather than actually buy the stock. If you're interested in more information regarding stock trading, please feel free to contact me and I can provide you with more information. But ignore those other kinds for now. **What you want is a cash account.**

Okay, next we need to talk about tax deferral. Most likely, you'll have heard of either a 401(k) account, an IRA or Individual Retirement Account or an RRSP or Registered Retirement Savings Plan account if you're in Canada.

Before I go on, I need to run through a disclaimer:

> *I, Dan Christian Yeung, am a guy who knows a lot about how to get rich and financially independent. However, I am not a certified financial planner or advisor. As such, any investment decisions that you make, whether or not as a result of any advice contained within this book; on* savemoneybuildwealth.com; *or contained within an emailing from* savemoneybuildwealth.com, *are made ultimately at your own risk.*

If you're an American, you should open up what's called a "Roth IRA." If you are Canadian, you should open up a TFSA (Tax Free Savings Account). A Roth IRA and TFSA are similar. Contributions to both of these accounts are after-tax money (you don't get a refund check from the government as you would with a traditional IRA or RRSP). Both offer tax-free growth (you don't need to pay income tax on money you make within these accounts). One of the major differences between the two is that you can withdraw money out of a TFSA without paying tax, but you can only withdraw your initial contributions from your Roth IRA without paying tax, not the profit. But, I don't want this money to stay as cash in these accounts forever, that's why I specifically state that your new $10,000 account be either a Roth IRA or a TFSA.

Oh yeah, I called this your new $10,000 account. Transfer over all the money from your current $10,000 account to your new $10,000 account once your new $10,000 account is set up.

Summary

This chapter gave you a bit of an introduction to what you can expect in this section of the book. I'm going to go over what investments and assets you should buy depending on how much money is in your $10,000 account. I also talked a bit about brokerage accounts and what you should buy. The next chapter is going to go into what investments you should be looking at.

If you haven't already done so, please visit *savemoneybuildwealth.com* and subscribe. The information on *savemoneybuildwealth.com* is more up-to-date. Plus, the website has free extras that will help you get even closer to your financial goals.

$ 0-10,000 Cash Index ETF's

Compounding

When you go to open your brokerage account, you might need to put in a minimum amount. Some places have no minimum requirement. Other places can have as much as a $3000 minimum. It's okay if you don't have the money invested right now; however I would like you to start investing money as soon as you can. The biggest reason? **Compounding.**

What is compounding?

There are just some things about investing that are truly magical. One such thing is the magic of compounding. The investments that I'm going to be talking about in a bit will earn you about 8% per year. Sometimes you'll make a little bit more, and sometimes you make a little bit less, but in general you will earn 8% per year. So, if you start out

> "There are just some things about investing that are truly magical."

with $1000, at the end of the year you'll end up with $1080. It makes sense that you'll make $80 per year on $1000.

But, in year two you're not going to start out with $1000. You're going to start it with $1080. $1080 invested at 8% will make you $86.40, $6.40 more than he made the year before. You're going to start at your third year with $1166.40. That amount invested at 8% will leave you $1259.71. In your third year you'll make $93.31,

$13.31 more than you made at the end of year one. This is because you had more money to start out with at the beginning of year three.

Let's fast-forward. Let's assume that we have been doing this for twenty-five years. At the end of year twenty-five, you'll have $6848.48, and you'll have made $507.29 over the course of year twenty-five.

Compounding does take a while to get going, but when it's does, you make money really quickly.

With the above example, we haven't added any additional money. We started with $1000 and we just reinvested the profit and any dividends. Let's see what happens if we were to add an additional $1000 per year. At the end of year two, you'll have $2246.40 in your account. At the end of year ten, you'll have $15,645.49 in your account. At the end of twenty-five years, you'll have $78,954.42 in your account! Imagine if you were able to find a way to save $1000 per year and invest it at 8% in the course of twenty-five years. And I haven't even told you the good stuff yet!

So, it's okay to let the cash in your $10,000 account sit for now, but it's ideal to start compounding as soon as possible.

Assets

Certain things are okay for you to buy with the money in your $10,000 account, and other things you should stay away from. If you know me personally or remember from earlier in this book, I absolutely detest mutual funds.

The things that I want you to buy are what I call "assets."

If you've taken any financial course in school, you've probably learned that an asset is an object that you own. You probably learned that a house is an asset, a car is an asset, your computer is an asset, probably even your smart phone is an asset. Of course money investments are assets as well.

This is pretty inaccurate.

The information, mindset, knowledge, and habits that you picked up through school and other education have gotten you to where you are. School taught you a definition of the word "assets," but that definition is not entirely correct.

So, what is an asset?

An asset is an instrument or a system that pays you to own it. The only way your house is an asset is if you rent it out and you make rental income and that rental income is more than your expenses. Even if you have equity in your home (i.e. you owe less than it's worth), unless your house is paying you money in your bank account, it's a liability. An investment that pays you money on a regular basis is an asset. Money, if you lend it out to somebody else and that somebody else pays you for the privilege of utilizing that money, is an asset.

So, use that money in your $10,000 account to buy assets. Use that money to buy something that pays you to own it.

With that said, you might ask this question:

Is a good financial edu ation an asset?

By this, I mean a Bob Proctor seminar or a Jack Canfield Course or an Internet marketing mastermind or a real estate investing luncheon. Does education pay you to own it? If you get good quality education, and you put it to good use, it'll pay you ten to a hundred times more than what you paid for it. This also goes for good coaching.

So, if you want to use the money from your $10,000 account to buy education from some of the greats that will help you achieve your financial goals, either in the form of books or coaching or audio courses, I fully endorse it. Go ahead and do it! Go learn real estate investing and go learn internet marketing! Invest in yourself.

If you're interested in pursuing coaching or mastermind sessions, please feel free to email me at dan@savemoneybuildwealth.com. I also suggest watching the movie *The Secret*. Any one of the financial courses or other trainings offered by any of the teachers on *The Secret* will be of good quality.

The Stock Market

If you know what the stock market is, you can probably skim through this section. A stock market is pretty much like any other market. If you visit the farmer's market, you'll probably encounter a bunch of farmers selling various goods like fruits or vegetables or other handmade goodies. If you visit a stock market, you'll encounter people who buy or sell or trade percentages of or "shares" of ownership in companies that are listed in that particular stock market. In the United States, there's a bunch of different stock markets. You've likely heard of most of these—the New York Stock Exchange, the NASDAQ, the Chicago Stock Exchange, and a bunch of others. In Canada, we have the Toronto Stock Exchange (TSX), the TSX Venture Exchange, the Montréal Exchange, and the Canadian Securities Exchange, again among others.

> **"The fact of the matter is that people who invest long term fair better than those who invest short term."**

I'm not going to go too much into how to pick stocks because I'm, by no means, a professional stock picker, though I've done pretty well on a few trades. The fact of the matter is that people who invest long term (ten years plus) fair better than those who invest short term (as much as two years or as little as two minutes). If you want to use a small portion of your $10,000 account to buy stocks, go for it. There's quite a bit of education out there on how to buy stocks and how to evaluate companies. For me, I look at two things. I look at something called technicals and I look at something called fundamentals. The technicals of a stock describe how the stock has mathematically performed and determine, based on past performance, whether or not the stock should go up or go down in value.

The fundamentals of a stock are who's the CEO, who are the board members, what decisions are they making, what new products are they inventing or going to come out with, what might the spend money on next, and details like that. For me, I may buy a stock if it has recently gone down in value but the reason why makes sense, and I know that that negative event will soon be rectified. Also, I may buy a stock if I see that the book value of the stock is higher than the market price of the stock. The book value of the company is how much equity it has, and you can divide this amount by the amount of shares that are outstanding.

But, here's what I know about buying and trading stocks: if you can be right 55% of the time, you can make it big on Wall Street. It takes a lot of effort, training, agony, and working through a lot of fear in order to be good enough to be right 55% of the time. Some ways to buy stocks alleviate a lot of the risk. One way is to only buy blue chip stocks. Blue chip stocks or blue chip companies are huge companies that you know are not going to go away anytime soon. Blue chip stocks are like McDonald's stocks, MasterCard stocks, Coca-Cola stocks, and Disney stocks. If a big crash or recession happens, if these companies are affected at all, they'll be less affected than some of the smaller or riskier companies.

The other way to alleviate the risk of buying stocks is to buy a whole bunch of different stocks. If you buy a whole bunch of stocks, then if a certain sector or certain company tanks, then only a certain percentage of your portfolio loses value.

One trade (i.e. purchasing one or more stocks in a company in one transaction) in your $10,000 account shouldn't cost more than $10, but if you're going to buy a whole bunch of stocks from different companies, you'll have to pay the commission fee ($10 likely) for each different company. One way to get around this is to purchase a mutual fund.

Mutual funds

Ah, yes, mutual funds. In theory mutual funds are actually not a bad idea. A mutual fund gives investors who don't have a lot of money but still want to invest into a bunch of different stocks, bonds, commodities, and other financial instruments a way to do so. What happens is a bunch of investors who don't have a lot of money combine all their money together and then buy the bunch of stocks together. This way, you get the benefits of investing the same as someone who has a lot of money and who has the money to buy a bunch of different stocks.

But remember I don't like mutual funds.

I'll tell you why. When this bunch of investors combines their money together, this money needs to be managed by somebody. Also, most likely this bunch of investors are mostly comprised of people that either have not done a lot of research into the stock market or are not interested at all in any kind of market research. They want to rely on a portfolio manager.

This portfolio manager's job, in theory, is to do a whole bunch of market research and assemble mutual funds based on the preferences and the risk tolerance of their clients. Clients who want to focus on long-term wealth are steered towards portfolios and baskets of stocks that offer long, steady but slow growth. Clients who want their money back in a couple years and want to make a lot of money within those couple years are steered towards high-risk, high-reward baskets of stocks.

The portfolio manager's job is to also outperform the market average. Since this person is supposed to have their ear to the ground and be tuned to ever-changing market conditions, their portfolios are supposed to do better than the average stock on the stock market. However, this is hardly ever the case.

In the beginning of March 2015, CNN reported that 86% of portfolio managers failed to beat the market average. As odd as this sounds, this is not an uncommon trend. If you don't believe me, look it up on Google. Most portfolio managers actually don't beat the market average. The people that do beat the market are the people that don't make it their goal. The fund managers that focus on other goals such as matching a stock market index or following a commodity trend such as an oil trend outperform those who are just trying to make as much money as possible.

There's another major reason why I don't like mutual funds.

The average commission on a mutual fund is 2% to 3%. So, if your mutual fund goes up by 5% in a given year, you have to pay 2% to 3% of that to your fund manager, and you only get to keep the remaining 2% to 3%. If you mutual fund goes down by 5% in a given year, you still have to pay 2% to 3% of that to your fund manager and you're down 7% to 8% of your hard-earned money.

You know the person that set up your brokerage account if you went to a big bank? You know the person that tried selling you mutual funds and other financial instruments? I don't know if you know this, but that person is actually a salesperson and makes money if you end up buying the mutual funds that the bank offers.

So, I'm telling you to stay away from stocks and to stay away from mutual funds. Why did I get you to open a brokerage account?

Exchange traded funds (ETFs)

Yeah, ETF's. I love these babies! If you can't afford to own a bunch of different stocks, what you can do is buy one or a couple of ETF's. A typical ETF is comprised of a basket of different stocks, bonds, commodities, and other financial instruments.

But isn't that a mutual fund?

You're right, I kind of described a mutual fund, but that's where the similarities end.

You see, you buy a mutual fund from either a bank or a financial institution. You deal with the company, and then that company turns around and manages it. If you want to get your money out of the mutual fund, the bank or financial institution needs to turn around and sell shares on your behalf, and then disperse the money to you. This process usually takes a couple of days, and of course, the bank or the financial institution will make a pretty healthy profit from the transaction for their services and their trouble.

When you buy an ETF, there's no middleman. You're dealing with a guy who's right on the trading floor. If you want to get money out of your ETF, as long as the stock market is open, you can get your money right away.

Some ETF's out there have as little as a 0.3% management fee.

Most importantly, most ETF's are not designed to beat the market, they're designed to track or meet the market. Most ETF's are comprised of a few of the biggest companies within a certain stock market or stock exchange or stock index.

So, because the person managing an ETF is only trying to track an index or a market and the person is most likely on the trading floor, you'll be able to take advantage of a much lower fee.

Index ETFs

Now that you know that you should be buying ETF's, you're going to need to know what kind of ETF's to buy. You can get a whole lot of different ETF's. You can get ETF's that track markets all over the world. You can get ETF's that track gold, silver, oil, the Russian Stock Exchange, Brazil. You name it.

Let's take a step back. Let's take a look at stock markets in general. The stocks within a certain large well-established stock market will fluctuate in value. They'll go up and down. New companies will get listed on the market, and other companies will get de-listed or go bankrupt. But, well-established markets have been around for a pretty long time. With all the time and money and effort spent on analysing stocks within stock markets, it probably makes sense that each market has what's called an average or a number which reflects how the stocks within a market are generally doing. It shouldn't be surprising that this number does exist; it's called an index.

"Over the past hundred years plus, the S&P 500 and the TSX has increased in value by 7 to 8% per year. This includes all the crashes, the bubbles, and the booms."

A stock market index is a number which generally reflects how well the average stock or how the bigger stocks are faring. Each of the markets have their own index, but analysts also like to make up their own indices. An example of such an index is called the S&P 500. The S&P 500 is a number which reflects how the average of the top 500 companies listed on the New York Stock Exchange or the NASDAQ are doing. In Canada, we have something called a TSX Composite Index. The TSX Composite Index is a reflection of how the top

70% of the companies listed on the TSX are doing on average. We also have the TSX 500 and the TSX 60. You can probably guess what these indices represent.

Here's a cool fact. Over the past hundred years plus, the S&P 500 and the TSX has increased in value by 7 to 8% per year. This includes all the crashes, the bubbles, and the booms. I cannot say for certain, but most likely the S&P 500 and the TSX are going to continue to grow on average by 7 to 8% per year.

So, buy Index ETF's. If you're in the United States, by an ETF that tracks the S&P 500. In Canada, by an ETF that tracks either the TSX Composite Index, or what I actually do is buy an ETF that tracks how the big six banks are doing.

Because ticker symbols may change and new products become available on the market, and I actually don't know when you are reading this book, I've listed the ETF's that you should buy on *savemoneybuildwealth.com*. Please feel free to Google Index ETF's, look up the ticker symbols, and purchase these. Or, if you're in Canada, as long as the major six banks (Bank of Montréal, TD Canada Trust, Bank of Nova Scotia, Royal Bank, Canadian Imperial Bank Of Commerce, and National Bank) are still written into the Constitution, bank ETF's work just fine as well.

How do you buy an ETF?

Oh, I should probably cover this. If you've bought stocks before, you could probably skip this. If you haven't done it before, you will want to log into your brokerage account, find the search box, and type in the ticker symbol of the ETF you want to buy. Once it shows up, you'll want to take stock of the current market value. Because ETF's trade like stocks, the value may vary on a continual basis. Divide the amount of money you have available to buy ETF's by the current market value and round down. Take note of this number.

Click on the "buy" button. You'll get a screen which says how many shares you want to buy, and if you want to buy at the market price or a different price (like a limit price). Buy the number of shares that you noted in the previous step. Because you're not day trading, it's okay to buy at the current market value. Click next and finish until you've officially bought the ETF.

If you feeling nervous, just remember you're using newfound money that you would've otherwise not had if you hadn't read this book. If you lose all this money (which is very unlikely) you won't be any worse off than before you started this process, and if anything you've done something you've never done before and you've gained experience.

Summary

Hopefully, I was able to give you some insight as to what you should be buying when you first start out on your investment journey. You may be tempted to buy stocks that your friends and associates tell you to buy. If you actually go ahead and do that, it's fine, as long as you do it with a very small portion of your $10,000 account. For now, you would be wise to allocate most of your $10,000 account into Index ETF's. Index ETF's aren't as sexy as stocks which can double or triple in value over the course of the year, but you're more likely to get an 8% yearly return on an index ETF then on a non-blue-chip stock.

Also, remember compounding! Compounding is very powerful. It's better to start compounding now with a lower amount then wait ten years and start compounding even if you are starting out with more than you did before. Just for a quick example, if you save $500 per year over the course of twenty-five years at 8% per year, at the end of year twenty-five you'll have $39,477.21. If you start ten years later, even if you manage to save $1000 per year as opposed to $500 per year, you'll only end up with $29,324.28 at the end of year fifteen.

Build the habit and start compounding early. Also, if your ETF pays you dividends in your $10,000 account, use that money to buy more of the same ETF if you're not planning to buy another asset or education with the dividends.

In the next chapter, I'm going to be talking about what to invest in once we start building up that money. ETF's are only going to return about 8% on a yearly basis, so we're going to want you to start buying and investing in assets that will return more than 8% per year.

Remember, if you have not visited *savemoneybuildwealth.com*, visit it as soon as you can! And subscribe. The information on *savemoneybuildwealth.com* is more up-to-date than the information within this book, and the bonuses that you can get are invaluable.

$ 10,000-25,000 Private Lending

What private lending is

Private lending is where you lend your money to somebody else and that other person pays back interest as well as the original amount that you lent out within a given timeframe. Most often this is for a real estate purchase, but this can also be for purchasing other items such as a car or a boat or even for buying a business. Banks make billions of dollars lending out money to other people so they can do things like buy cars and buy houses. A lot of people don't know this, but you do now because you're reading it here, you can do the same thing with your money.

More often than not, if you look hard enough on Craigslist or Kijiji you'll come across somebody or a family who is trying to buy a house but needs to quickly clean up credit card debt in order to be approved for their mortgage. They often need $3000 or $10,000 to be paid off so it's removed from their credit report. Because they're are already stretching to just get the minimum down payment, they'll often not have the money they need to clean up the credit card. So they need somebody to lend them money in a way that will not show up on their credit report.

Enter you. You have this money in your $10,000 account. It is very reasonable for you to charge a fee of 20 to 30% for short-term loan such as this. Of course what you'll want to do is broker an agreement through a lawyer. Make sure that you get some collateral or a piece of the property they're purchasing if you don't get your principal plus your interest back. You can get the borrower to cover the costs of the lawyer or you can use part of the 20 to 30% profit to pay for the lawyer. One of my real estate mentors does this on a regular basis.

Another type of private lending, as I mentioned before, is lending money to people or companies that are trying to acquire or renovate real estate. These entities will likely need a loan over the span of a year to update their property, and then what they'll do is they'll take out a reverse mortgage or a line of credit based on the future value of their property. I like this type of investing. I really think you should consider it as well because these people need to pay their lenders or creditors (you) first. If they default on their interest payments or in paying back your original loan amount, you'll get a piece of the property that they registered the loan against.

If this sounds really complicated to you, companies will facilitate this for you. In Canada, examples of such companies include ProFunds and Paramount Equity Financial Corporation. In the United States, one such company is the Lending Club. With the Lending Club, you can buy notes for as low as $2500 (a note in loan terms is a contract which specifies when a loan must be repaid and what the interest is).

Companies such as Paramount screen and ensure that the entities seeking a private loan have decent credit and have collateral just in case a default occurs. If a borrower defaults, the company taking collateral also loses out, so it's beneficial for them to make sure that the borrower is of the highest quality possible.

Another private lending investment vehicle available to you is what's called a syndicate mortgage. A syndicate mortgage is where you and a bunch of other people lend money to a real estate developer to buy land for their development. An example of a company that does this is Greybrook. See, getting a mortgage to construct a building and pay for the labor is pretty easy to do. Getting a bank loan to buy a large chunk of land is nearly impossible (at least in Canada). So, what real estate developers do is they assemble investors to help put together the money required to buy the piece of land and then the investors get paid out once the property that the real estate developer is developing gets sold. The massive disadvantage is once you lend money to this type of developer, you likely won't see any returns for five years. But, the massive advantage is, once the returns start piling in, they REALLY start to pile in! Including the five years of wait without any money coming in, you can pretty much expect to make at least a 20 to 25% per year return on your investment.

> **"I like to err on the side of caution, but I love to make as much money as possible."**

Why am I suggesting private lending? Everybody has their own investing style. Some people love the risk and love to take chances; other people want to play it as safe as possible. I like to err on the side of caution, but I love to make as much money as possible. Private lending done through the right companies has the same risk as the safer stocks on the stock market, but you can get a higher return on a shorter-term private loan than you can get in the stock market.

You can invest with other people's money, though I don't suggest doing this with stocks nor ETF's. If you have access to a line of credit, if you can find a way to lend out the money on that line of credit to somebody for a higher interest rate than the interest rate on the line of credit, you just found a way to create money out of thin air.

What other vehicles to consider at this stage

If you don't think private lending is for you, that's completely fine. It is okay to stick to investing in Index ETF's and compounding and trying to squeeze out even more money from your everyday purchases to put in your $10,000 account. Whether it is one year, five years, or even ten years, you're eventually going to get to the stage where you will actually have $10,000 in your $10,000 account. When this happens, you probably want to set a higher goal. Start referring to your $10,000 account as a $25,000 or $50,000 account. If you decide to take money out of this account to purchase an asset, do not rename your account to a lower amount. For instance, if you're calling it your $25,000 account, but you're taking out $25,000 to do a private loan or some coaching, don't start calling it a $10,000 account again. You can't move forward without going backwards.

Summary

Hopefully I've just opened your eyes to my version of the world of investing. When most people hear the word "investing," they think about stocks or mutual funds. My world of investing involves buying and owning assets. I think about buying stuff that pays me to own it. Money pays me to own it if it's earning interest, and it's most definitely earning interest if it's lent out to somebody and I can rest assured that the money will be returned back to me in a predetermined period of time.

In the next chapter, I'm going to talk about the mechanism that most millionaires use to achieve their wealth, and that's by actual real estate. If done the right way, real estate can give you mind-blowing returns. Plus, you can invest in real estate in so many ways. I've already discussed one way. That's to invest in a private mortgage or private loan. Well, when we get to actually buying real estate, you'll see how you can get a much higher return.

$ 25,000+
Real Estate

Real estate types

What I could tell you about real estate investing could fill up several books. Real estate investing can offer you the best of both worlds. You can get rich quick doing it if you want to take a high risk, or you can take a long time and be patient but have a really good chance of earning a lot of wealth over the long term. If you've never really looked into real estate investing before, I'm going to give you a bit of a crash course here, but if you really want to get into this I would suggest attending a detailed course or getting really good coaching from somebody who does this on a regular basis and has a lot of experience.

Let's start with two different strategies for buying physical real estate. You can do a fix and flip where you buy a distressed property, do a whole bunch of renovations, and sell it for way more than you originally bought the property plus the amount you spent on renovations. This is the get-rich-quick method. The risk is in not finding a buyer promptly or not finding a buyer who's willing to pay more than you spent on the purchase and the renovation.

The second strategy is to buy, fix, and hold. You buy a distressed property, you renovate it, and you hold onto it for a long time, renting it out in the process. You will get steady cash flow from the rental income, but you won't have as much cash in your hand at the end of the renovation as you would have if you flipped it.

Other strategies exist and even these two strategies have many,

63

many different variations, but these two are the main ones.

You can also buy many different investment properties. You can buy a single house or a single family property, you can buy a condominium, or you can buy a multifamily property where two or more living units are attached to each other. You can even buy commercial units or an entire strip mall. In general, you'll be able to get a better return buying multifamily properties than buying a single house, a single family property, or a single condominium within a condominium complex.

Financing

If you bought the house you're currently in, you're probably already familiar with how mortgages work. If not, you can probably guess that you approach your bank and ask them how much you can afford to spend on a house and how much of a down payment you would need to fork over.

Leverage
How to make money with real estate

Here's where real estate investing stands out from almost every other type of investment vehicle available. While it is true that you can borrow money to invest in stocks, if you go to your bank and ask for a loan to invest in stocks (called a "margin"), the bank will only loan you a certain percentage of the amount of money that you currently have in your brokerage account. As you know, when you buy a piece of property using a mortgage, you only need to put down a certain small percentage. Usually this number is 20%, but you can go as low as 5% or even 0% if you jump through the right hoops.

For example, let's say that you have $20,000 in your $25,000 account. If you want to buy stocks, and you believe in a stock so much that you think you'll be out ahead if you were to borrow money to buy the stock, the bank is only going to lend you maybe an additional $12,500 to do so.

Now, let's take a look at a house. I'm going to assume here that the house is in pretty good shape in a pretty good neighborhood and that you've agreed to a pretty reasonable purchase price. If you want to buy this house and you only have $20,000 in your $25,000 account, most banks will have no issue lending you the additional $80,000 or even $180,000 to purchase the house, assuming that you have decent credit. The funny part is the bank will lend you this money at an interest rate of about 3% (at the time of writing this book). As you can see, banks tend to see good quality real estate as a much more stable investment than stocks.

Does this matter?

This matters, and in a big way.

Again, continuing on with the crash course, buying and holding real estate doesn't just provide you one way of making money, it provides you with four ways of making money:

- Passive Appreciation
- Active Appreciation
- Cash Flow
- Principle Recapture

Passive appreciation describes how much your property goes up in value every year. The passive appreciation rate of the average property in the United States and Canada (save for the housing crash) is somewhere around 3% per year. If you spend $100,000 on a house, the house on average will appreciate in value by about 3% per year, so it will actually appraise at $103,000 after a year. If you remember what I said about compounding earlier, you'll know that it will appraise higher than $106,000 after two years.

Active appreciation is where you actively do a renovation and force the value of your property to go up. Like, if you were to swap out the light fixtures or update the washrooms, you could likely increase the value of your property by way more than you spend on your renovation.

Cash flow is how much money you have left after your renter pays you and after your expenses. It's a simple calculation.

Principle recapture is how much of the rent payment goes to pay the non-interest part of the mortgage.

So, if your mortgage is $800 per month, and $400 of that is interest and the other $400 pays back the loan, the $400 that pays back the loan is actually profit (as long as it's your renter paying it).

Isn't that cool? Conventional real estate investments provide you with FOUR different ways to profit!

But, that's not the coolest part about real estate investing!

Are you ready for this? I love this part!

Remember "compounding"? There's another word, and this word is so, so, so much better!! It's called:

Leverage.

Okay, I think the best way for me to explain leverage is to use an example. I'll use one of my current rental properties.

I bought my property for $200,000 (It was actually lower but I'll say $200,000 because it's a round number). I'm currently renting it for $1600/month (It's actually higher, but again . . . round numbers etc.)

Here are my expenses (round numbers):

- Mortgage: $800/month ($400 interest, $400 principle recapture)
- Property Tax: $125/month
- Condo Fee: $250/month
- Power/Cable/Internet: $125/month
- Total expenses: $1,300/month ($400 is principle recapture)

Okay, so here are the profit numbers for me:

- Passive appreciation at 3%: **$6,000**
- Active appreciation: $0 (didn't renovate it)
- Cash flow: $300/month times 12 months = **$3,600**
- $1,600 - $800 - $125 - $250 - $125 = $300
- Principle recapture: $400 times 12 months = **$4,800**
- Total profit: $6,000 + $3,600 + $4,800 = **$14,400**

$14,400 / $200,000 = 7.2% per year.

Not bad, the average stock market return is about 7-8% per year. Private lending will have a better return though. But, can you see what's wrong with this picture?

I didn't pay $200,000 for the property.

I only paid $20,000!

I only put down 10%. I got a mortgage for the other $180,000.

Let's take a second look at the numbers. I paid $20,000, and got a profit of $14,400 in one year. That means...

I got a 72% return on my investment in the first ear alone!!

67

Why? **Leverage**. I leveraged someone else's money (i.e. the bank's), and while the bank is getting 2.5% on my mortgage, I'm getting 72% on my property!

You can leverage real estate at 3% interest (again at the time of writing this book). You can't do this with stocks or even private lending. If you are serious about building wealth, definitely consider acquiring some income properties.

How to go about buying real estate

Finding the proper piece of real estate takes a lot of searching. You'll probably end up searching for and analysing hundreds of properties before you finally find one that will produce the income that you are looking for.

In the previous section, I mentioned that there are four ways to profit from buying and holding real estate. One of these methods is passive appreciation, but if you can get a vendor (seller) to sell you the property for lower than the property is actually worth, you'll be able to start out with a pretty good chunk of passive appreciation.

If I can give you just one piece of advice when it comes to buying any piece of real estate, not just an income property, make sure you ask your real estate agent this or try to figure out this information about a property that you're analysing:

Why is the vendor selling the property?

I see a lot of people analyse real estate, and they use *a lot* of information. They look at some really crazy metrics and trends and do some intense statistical analysis and forecasting. I've also been through my fair share

> "Very few people actually ask why the vendor is selling the property."

of real estate courses. But, very few people actually ask why the vendor is selling the property. If you want to buy property for way less than it's actually worth, find out why the vendor is selling the property AND find a way to satisfy his or her need. I've seen people use plane tickets as a down payment. Sometimes the people are selling their house because they need to downsize or move into a long-term care facility.

Rather than just doing the typical negotiation through your real estate agent or realtor, why not offer to help move the vendor into their long term care facility in return for a lower purchase price? If the vendor is selling her property because she's very frustrated about cleaning up after her tenants on a regular basis and she just absolutely does not want to be a landlord anymore, why not approach her that day with cash and an offer to buy the property as is? Be creative. It kind of scares me knowing how many real estate agents out there don't actually know why their clients are selling their properties.

Speaking in general terms, you'll want to look for areas with low vacancy rates, lower property costs, but higher rent rates. You will also probably want to stay away from areas which have higher crime rates. You'll probably want to gravitate towards neighborhoods that have lots of younger families. As long as your home town or city has a strong economy, the first rental property you should buy should be close to where you live. If you currently live in a house and you have the ability to turn your basement into a rental suite, this would be the ideal place for you to start.

If you can afford to buy a multifamily building, this is much better than buying a single house. If you have a single house, and it's vacant, you're bringing in zero income. If you have a multifamily building, even if one or a few of the units are vacant, you're still bringing in income from the units that are occupied.

Also if you're able to find a multifamily building that has four or more rental units, you can probably qualify for commercial financing. This means that the bank doesn't look at your personal credit to determine whether or not you qualify for financing. Instead, the bank looks at the rental potential of the building that you looking to purchase and determines whether or not you qualify for a mortgage based on the potential of the building alone. The downside to this though is usually 35% down is required to qualify for commercial financing, and commercial financing interest rates are around the 5 to 7% range.

No money down

Don't have enough money in your $25,000 account to buy real estate? Then don't use your own money! Find another person who is willing to lend you money to buy real estate.

Remember earlier on when I was talking about private lending and private mortgages? You can also take out a private loan and use that as a down payment. Or you could go out and find people who have more than enough money to invest in real estate but currently have their money invested in things such as mutual funds that are barely breaking even. You can approach these people and show them how much money they can make doing real estate. Not everyone would be excited about the prospect of making a 72% return in one year, but I'm pretty sure at least one or two people just might. What you do is that, once you have a property that you know is a homerun, you start approaching people and show them how much money they can make, and you ask if you can split the profits. They'll provide the money, you'll do pretty much all the work in completing the purchase and finding tenants and collecting rent checks, and you split the profits. If, after splitting the profits 50-50, you're not able to beat your money partner's current investment returns with the property that you're looking at, you need to find a better property.

Mentors or clubs

As you can tell from the complexity of the past few pages, it is probably a good idea for you to take one or several real estate courses and find yourself a mentor or a support group before you actually start going out and buying properties. One of the keys to success, not just in real estate investing or getting rich, but for anything in life, is to find someone who has actually has been successful in doing what you want to do and then trying to learn from them and emulate them. If your dream is to open a hair salon, actually go out and find a salon owner and offer to take them to coffee or lunch. More often than not, you will find that most successful people are more than willing to share their wisdom with others. Don't worry at all about giving off the impression that you want to compete with them. They would rather help you than sit by and watch while you struggle down a road full of pitfalls they've already learned how to avoid. Who knows? One day you might end up being business partners or even friends!

Summary

Hopefully, I've been able to open your mind to ways that you actually can become rich or at least come out ahead financially. I've showed you ways to save money even if you have no money to save and how to invest that money so you can have either a pretty decent return or a really good return. I've even showed you how to acquire assets even if you have no money! You know, wealthy people do this all the time. They find ways to buy assets for little to no money, and they hire people to cultivate and turn these assets into really crazy moneymakers.

Next, I'm going to show you some other ways to make tons of money with little to no money to start with.

Also, if you haven't already done so, I urge you to visit *savemoneybuildwealth.com* and check out some of the articles and subscribe. My website has a lot of information that's going to be much more up-to-date than this book. The information on the website will go a long way to helping you achieve your financial goals.

Other Ways To Get Rich

Internet marketing

In the context of saving money and turning around to use that money to build wealth, the concept of Internet marketing or even direct mail marketing is almost an afterthought. But if this book was about how to double or triple the profits of your business or your practice, Internet marketing would be one of the first topics I'd mention.

Internet marketing is a really simple straightforward way to create money out of pretty much nothing. What you do is you find a bunch of people who are interested in a certain topic, you offer to give some something for free if they give you an email address, and you actually give them that thing once they give you their email address. This has probably happened to you quite often.

> "I'm not talking about spamming. I'm talking about giving your prospect useful information."

Once you have their email address, you can send them a bunch of emails afterwards. I'm not talking about spamming. I'm talking about giving your prospect useful information. You know that this person is likely interested in the topic because they asked for your free report or free video.

Some of these emails contain solutions or products that will solve the problem that your prospect probably has. These products or solutions might be products that your business has or is trying to sell, or it might be someone else's products. If you're selling someone else's products, you're what's called an "affiliate."

The difference between sending of these emails and sending out what's called "spam" is that spam is generic, unsolicited email sent to a bunch of different email addresses. I'm asking you to send out an email only to somebody who gave you their email address because they were interested in a product that you were either selling them or giving to them for free.

Another aspect of Internet marketing that I want to touch upon is what's called a "sales funnel." If you're selling somebody a product, and you're not upselling or downselling, you're leaving a lot of money on the table. If somebody is willing to buy your $7 product, maybe they'd be willing to buy your $70 product or even your $270 product. If 5% of your prospects buy your $7 dollar product also bought your $70 product and if 1% of these people bought your $270 product, you would be much further ahead than if you only provided your prospects a $7 product.

Lastly, if somebody bought something from you, make sure you capture their contact information and don't forget to sell them or try to sell them more products in the future. It's harder now than ever to get somebody to buy a product from you (that's why most vendors nowadays offer perspective customers something for free) but it is also easier now than ever to get a future sale from a current client. If somebody buys something from you (not just online but in person), but you don't collect their contact information, you're leaving a lot of money on the table. If somebody buys a greeting card from you, and they really liked it, you can gently remind them once in a while that you have other greeting cards they might be interested in. They might come back in the future and buy more cards from you. If you don't have their contact information, they may forget about you within the next couple days.

Start a business

I don't mean go out and buy a McDonald's or a restaurant and start working in it. I'm talking about, if you're good at Photoshop or if you're good at hemming wedding dresses or good at crafts, market these skills! Go on Craigslist or Kijiji and offer these skills to people! Use some of the advice in the previous section, and offer people a free service, and then upsell them more services. But make sure this is something you like doing and that you're good at.

Most people I know have a job doing what they don't want to do. They spend long hours being stressed out at their job and constantly being scared that they're going to get fired from it. It's pretty sad that a lot of us don't enjoy our work.

Most of us have a special talent or skill that we enjoy doing. This is something that we would do for free. If it's a service that helps other people, you really need to find a way to start monetizing it and eventually find a way to make a living from it. You can learn how to this. You just need to believe that you can, and you actually need to make the effort and start pursuing this.

> "It's actually better if lots of other people are successful doing what your special talent is."

This special talent or skill doesn't need to be unique either, by the way. It's actually better if lots of other people are successful doing what your special talent is. This way you can copy something. Just like how I told you that, when you buy your first few properties, make sure that you're seeking the advice of others who have done it successfully. You should also make sure that you find someone who is successful in using what your special talent is and try getting them to help you become successful doing what it is you want to do.

It's very tempting for you to want to venture out on your own. Especially if you found a niche and you find that no one else is doing it. You probably heard that 90% of new businesses fail within one year of opening. If your talent or special skill falls within an existing niche that is proven to be successful, you're more likely to be part of the 10%.

If you need extra income, I would much rather you pursue this route than actually go out and get a second job. It's tiring enough to have to work one job, working a second job will burn you right out. I would rather you spend some time and effort to figure out what your special skills are and what you love to do and then find a way to monetize that.

Write a book

What?

Yup that's correct. I did suggest that you write a book.

But I don't know enough about anything to write a book!

If this is the first thought that popped into your head, I just proved to you why you should write a book.

By thinking that you don't know enough about anything to write a book, you pretty much just affirmed the position that people who write books have a lot of knowledge. So, by that logic, if you actually go ahead and write a book, other people that know you or don't know you will naturally make the assumption that you have a lot of knowledge (whether or not you actually do).

What should your book be about?

While your book can be about anything, if you want to get rich by writing a book, your book should be on the topic of what we discussed in the previous section. It should be about that small business that you're thinking of starting up or about your special skill. It should be a self-help book. For example, if your special skill is you're very good at cleaning houses, your book should be about something related to cleaning houses or keeping the house clean or special techniques you can use to maintain that "new house" look. If you think you don't have enough information to write a book or you don't think you're smart enough to write a book, remember the people that will end up reading your book are people that don't have the knowledge you have. Your book can be for people who don't know how to clean a house, not for people who are good at cleaning houses. And even if someone who is good at cleaning houses reads your book, if your book is titled *10 Easy Ways to Keep a Clean and Happy Household*, that person is unlikely to know your ten ways.

How is having a book going to increase your income?

The most obvious way having a book will increase your income is that you can sell copies of your book. But, if that's your only objective, you're probably going to have a tough time. What you want to do is use your book to sell you.

You want your book to pretty much be a marketing brochure. Of course your book is going to have lots of helpful tips, and it's going to help your reader out lots, but at the end of the day you want your book to promote your business. Actually, if you want to stay at your job, writing a book about what you do at your job is a pretty easy way to stand out and help you get raises and promotions. Imagine if ten people are up for promotion, and you're the only person who has actually written and published a book on the topic. Who

"Actually, if you want to stay at your job, writing a book about what you do at your job is a pretty easy way to stand out."

do you think is going to stand out the most?

Okay, let's get back to how we can increase your income with a book. Let's assume for a minute that you're a hairdresser. When somebody asks you what you do for a living, you probably answer "I am a hairdresser." The "a" is bold for a reason. You don't know this, but if you use "a" when you state what you do for work or what you do for **"You're actually reading my 'business card' right now."** money, you're not really going to stand out. The person talking to you is not going to see you as a better or different hairdresser than any of the other hairdressers out there.

Now let's assume that you take my advice and you write a book about how to maintain that salon look for as long as possible. Let's see how the conversation looks now.

- **Other person:** "What do you do for living?"

- **You:** "I'm the hairdresser that helps you stay beautiful well after your spa appointment." Or even, "I'm the author of the book *Stay Beautiful! How to Stay Beautiful Well after Your Spa Appointment.*"

What you think of that? Do you think you just increased your chances of landing a new client? Actually, here's how I like to tell my clients to play out the conversation:

- **Other person:** "Wow! [...] Can I get your card?"

- **You:** "No. I don't have a card."

- **Other person:** "What do you mean you don't have a card?"

- **You:** "I have a book. Actually I think I might have a copy with me in my purse *[always carry one or two copies of your book with you]*, would you like me to autograph it for you?"

By the way, this type of book will have your contact information in it. I sometimes carry business cards with me, but I rarely do. My books serve as my business card. You're actually reading my "business card" right now.

Why is that? Well, when you hand your business card out at networking events, how many people do you think actually keep your business card? Here's a hint: What did you do with the business cards that other people handed you over the years?

Books have perceived value. You can't really give somebody a business card as a present, but you can give somebody a book as a present. Business cards (except my business cards) don't really give the other person much value, unless they really value your contact information. Books give value. If you subtract the cost of producing these free books from the amount of business they generate, I'm further ahead than the business that I've tried generating only by handing out business cards and sending people to my websites. It is actually cheaper for me to use my book as a business card then to use an actual business card.

You might be thinking that this is a really good idea, but you don't know where to start. The thought of writing a book is daunting enough, and how are you going to get it published?

Luckily for you, I have a solution to both of these problems. If you're interested in utilizing a program that will help you not only write a book, but write the right book for dramatically increasing your income and guaranteeing that your book will actually get done and that you will have a publisher, visit *savemoneybuildwealth. com/become-an-author*. Even if you're not interested in writing a book right now, it would be worth checking this site out. You can also just hop on your computer, open up a Word document, and start typing. But trust me that it's much easier just to go with this program. The program helps you not only write your book but also have it published, using only ten hours of your effort. Most people spend years writing a book. Imagine having a book that's really well-written, published, listed on Amazon, and in your hand using only ten hours of your time.

By the way, being able to call yourself an "author" gives you some amazingly surprising prestige. Most people consider writing a book a big accomplishment. When you complete this program and when you write your first book, you'll see how easy this is. But most people are afraid to start for whatever reason. Publishing and releasing a book is a newsworthy event. If a newspaper or TV or magazine company needs a hairdresser to interview, they're probably going to want to interview somebody who has written a book. Writing a book gives you instant credibility and gives the interviewer something to talk about.

If you're looking for partners, or money, or recognition from some big names, having a book gives you an amazing calling card. Instead of yourself as just "Mary the Hairdresser," now you're "Mary the Published Author."

You may or may not know Dr. John Gray. John is the author of the book *Men Are from Mars, Women Are from Venus*. John has a PhD, but he has gone on record to say that writing a book and having it published gives you more credibility than a PhD. He was having issues getting TV and radio interviews when he announced himself as having a PhD in psychology, but as soon as he announced himself the published author of *Men Are from Mars, Women Are from Venus*, all of a sudden he didn't have trouble getting radio or TV interviews.

Hopefully I've been able to explain to you the advantages of becoming a published author. If you're interested in becoming one, visit *savemoneybuildwealth.com/become-an-author*. Remember, I'm not asking you to buy anything right now. I'm just asking you to look into it. Remember what I said about action? You're definitely going to want to take action on this if you're at all interested in building wealth and getting rich.

Network with others

You probably have a group of people that you hang out with on a regular basis. You likely feel safe and comfortable hanging out with these people and enjoy talking to them about certain topics that you enjoy. I love sports so I love hanging out with people who also love sports. The problem is though that a lot of the people that love sports aren't where I am financially or where I want to be financially.

One of my mentors said that one of the easiest ways for me to increase my income is to start hanging out with people richer than I am.

If you want to break through and achieve your financial goals, you might want to do the same. If you don't know anyone to hang out with who is where you want to be or who has what you want to have, look up groups. Visit *meetup.com* and look for groups to join, or join a mastermind.

If you have a business, one of the most powerful ways for you to ramp up your income is to join a mastermind. A mastermind is a group of five or six people that's usually led by somebody who is much further ahead either financially or spiritually than the rest of the group. What happens is each person in the mastermind takes turns sharing where they are and where they want to be and what their obstacles are. The rest of the people help this person solve their problem or break through their obstacles. Masterminds usually meet once every week or two weeks. Mastermind sessions usually last about an hour. With the Internet, you don't even need to be in the same country as your mastermind partners during your mastermind session.

If you're a salon owner for instance, don't you think it would be very powerful for you to mastermind with a few other salon owners and have a session led by someone who is very successful in the business arena?

Next steps

Congratulations for making it to the end of this book! The information you've digested will not only help you save money on your everyday purchases, but also help you get your finances in order, become wealthy, and even live the life that you actually want to live.

But what have you done so far? Have you set up your $10,000 account? Are you transferring money to this $10,000 account at the beginning of every month? Do you know how much you currently spend on a regular basis? Have you bought index funds? **Have you subscribed to** *savemoneybuildwealth.com* **and have you collected your free extras?**

One of the major differences between those who are wealthy and those who aren't wealthy is that the wealthy took action. When they got some very powerful advice, they acted upon it.

This book has a lot of good advice in it, but if I can give you one last piece of advice, don't stop learning. Don't ever stop learning. Education does not end at the conclusion of a degree or a book. Life is always changing, and you can either adapt or you can be left behind.

Eric Hoffer has an amazing quote:

> *"In times of change learners inherit the earth; while the learned find themselves beautifully equipped to deal with a world that no longer exists."*

I've listed a number of books at the end of this chapter that I really, **really** recommend that you read. I have more reading material on *savemoneybuildwealth.com* that I think you should take a look at as well. Also, if you haven't seen it yet, watch the movie *The Secret*.

Plus, sign up for mentorship and coaching in areas that you really want to pursue. If you don't know what you want to do, look at some of the courses that are offered by the teachers in *The Secret*. You should have the money for this in your $10,000 account.

I'm very grateful that you supported me by giving me the chance to share my wisdom with you, and I'm grateful for the opportunity to hopefully help you see the world in a slightly different way and provide you with some options that you otherwise would not have known were available to you.

Good luck and I really wish you happiness, health, and financial security.

Dan Christian Yeung

Dan Christian Yeung

Suggested Reading

You can find an updated list on savemoneybuildwealth.com/resources

- *The 4-Hour Workweek: Escape 9-5, Live Anywhere, and Join the New Rich* by Timothy Ferriss
- *The Success Principles - 10th Anniversary Edition: How to Get from Where You Are to Where You Want to Be* by Jack Canfield
- *Think and Grow Rich* by Napoleon Hill
- *Double Your Income Doing What You* Love by Raymond Aaron

About The Author

Dan Christian Yeung is the award winning author of *Dealership Deceit*. Dan has committed his life to teaching people just like you how to save money and achieve any financial goal. Using his own innovative techniques, he shows you step-by-step how to do all this without cutting back on your current lifestyle or on what you purchase on a regular basis!

www.ingramcontent.com/pod-product-compliance
Lightning Source LLC
Chambersburg PA
CBHW061836220326
41599CB00027B/5302